Dysplasia

poems by

Lucy Tiven

Finishing Line Press
Georgetown, Kentucky

Dysplasia

ACKNOWLEDGMENTS

Journals & publications in which the poems in this collection first
appeared:

*Front Porch, Fruita Pulp, Two Serious Ladies, HTMLGiant Sunday Service,
The Scrambler, Pop Serial, Lazy Fascist Review, Oddball Magazine, The
Quietus, What Weekly, Country Music, Everyday Genius, Vitriol, Metazen.*

Publisher: Leah Maines

Editor: Christen Kincaid

Cover Art: Neha Talreja

Author Photo: Mike Harris

Cover Design: Elizabeth Maines

Printed in the USA on acid-free paper.
Order online: www.finishinglinepress.com
also available on amazon.com

Author inquiries and mail orders:
Finishing Line Press
P. O. Box 1626
Georgetown, Kentucky 40324
U. S. A.

Table of Contents

To be a good human being is to have a kind of openness to the world, an ability to trust uncertain things beyond your own control, things that can lead you to be shattered in very
extreme circumstances for which you were not to blame.
That says something very important about the ethical life:
It is based on a trust in the uncertain and on a willingness to be exposed.
Trust is based on being more like a plant than like a jewel—something fragile but whose very particular beauty is inseparable from that fragility.

–Martha Nussbaum

America is a very spiritual place

–Eileen Myles

like this

when I burnt my fingertip
it was because I wanted to turn the
candle into a tiny trashcan. because I
don't know how to make people pay
attention to me without acting
like a wastebin set on fire
outside the park

like   people need
something for people to
swerve around and then
video with their phone

like   there is a voice
inside you that you actually
can't turn off by arching
your feet

the lamp I ordered from
eBay turned out to be a
dollhouse lamp.
you have to order a tiny
adaptor to make it plug into
a usual outlet. it sucks.

I still want to be a doll though

Repeat Offender

The middle of this movie
always makes me feel like rewinding it
all the way back to the beginning. I don't want
everything—just for this one dance
not to feel like a backwards-walking
competition. Maybe a taller roof,
somewhere to keep track of the sky
and those vanity plates at the same
time. An open relationship
is something one should aspire
to with the moon. It's thoughts
like these that keep me
uptight. I only say I'm
laughing when I'm laughing.
And I don't think anyone
should ever let themselves be
turned into the other person,
should let that damp light pass
through them, that thing you
think you've traded
disappointment in for until it
arrives. It arrives. I'm not
jealous but if I was, I would be
jealous of those trees that only
get to exist for one ecstatic
second of snow on film. Not
some woman. How they live
such a long time but not
forever.

A Poem in Which No One Is Named Bob

In a conversation with my therapist
I referred to you as Bob. Your name is not Bob obviously
and upon thinking to call you Bob I quickly wished
that I had picked a more imaginative fill in.

My therapist, whose name is not Bob either
said no one is named Bob anymore
at least not like they used to be—
I had a grandfather named Bob

until he was incinerated
and spread among Long Island Sound
a context in which it would be absurd
to refer to him as Bob or anything.

"Look, there is Bob drifting towards
a docked boat! And Bob, a fleck
of ash bobbing beside the pools
of moss and plastics!"

"Lucy, we have to separate reality
from the stories we tell ourselves,"
my therapist said, probably still thinking
not of my misplaced sentimentality for "Bob"
but of the popularity of children's names
in various periods of the 20th century,

"I think you cause yourself to suffer
because you feel inconsequential
to Bob," he said. "But you have to realize
that attributing your pain to Bob is a construction."

He seemed to suggest that the falsity of Bob
was a great ship I had built and set on fire
without realizing it. Outside, snow
was burying the recycling bins
waiting by the curb of the Student Health Center.
I thought of this, and of this poem
which is a construction too.

Westchester County

Can you believe that William Faulkner's grave plot
is the most expensive one on eBay
and it isn't even in a good neighborhood?
I've been drafting letters to Alice Cooper.

He was my grandmother's tennis partner
at the sanitarium. No one in my family remembers
its name, just the small room she shared
with an even smaller, older woman.

There is no record of Alice Cooper's stay in White Plains
as a mental patient either. So why bother.
I'm hearing things. I lie awake. Hello.
What do I call you. Why does my heart
make that sound. Is it trying to cut in.

Then, the same dry, altered light
in the morning. For you too.
She looked like Greta Garbo.
I do not. But beauty is
as beauty does. Haven't you heard?

deflected light

fields of questions

questions with public restrooms unlocked inside them

question-mansions

questions quietly rowing themselves out of the way

oblivious, homemade questions
tiny questions

questions that turn themselves in
questions ending with more questions

love questions

the piece of land your email address turned up in

after the moon got just too big
for anything else to get past

So Tragic

Long story short: he left. Sadness came after.
Long story long: There was mist
then strong wind, then a movie
about deep love & codes.

*

Thank you for the liturgy of engaging pains,
I should have said. *I did not think they would end.*

He spoke with a fractured mathematics
that takes time to ferment into coy realism.
If I drive close enough to the ocean at night,
it is sort of like being there.

*

Melancholia meaning: first, loving
& then loving pain. At least,
that's how it is for me. Icy lights
flickering onto the dock.
They look so cold
and don't feel it.

Forever Lover

Who knew water could bruise
like that. I used to even miss you
while I was explaining the premise
of "The Doggone Girl is Mine" to my parents

or watching the ending of an in-flight film
thinking for the whole movie
that the movie was almost over. I showed Leo
the place where my leg hit the Seine

the night I jumped off the bridge.
He told me I was crazy, putting a door
in place. He said I could have died. His job
was to build new things that looked old

enough to install into old houses. The town
was so small and everything felt small
inside it. He never wanted to leave
and pointed out the North star. I shrugged, told him
it was no good to me. Both of them

love this same woman but won't wise up
and realize she has no loyalty. I was driving past a salt flat
when you told me about the other girl you loved

and how you hurt her. I almost ruined my phone
with iced tea and it barely made it
into the passenger seat. From somewhere
there was a honk. I guess I thought
I would always be that person. It's a funny song
if you've never heard it before,

but now it mostly comes on when I'm stalled
in freeway traffic, tired, not knowing what to feel.
When I heard Michael Jackson was dead
we had just made love and dust was falling

softly from the ceiling. You rolled over,
covered yourself with part of a shirt
and turned on the radio. I did not know
what to feel then either.

cancel ticket please refund

quick. I'm thinking of a number. I wouldn't usually ask
but please. Ben. Can I borrow your wet trousers.
No reason. I'm not one of those girls who falls asleep
on other peoples laundry, I just like watching you buy milk
you drunken goon. And you still haven't told me
who's the biggest bathroom hog in your family? I like
making people do what I say. repeat three times fast:
cancel ticket please refund cancel ticket peas reflub can
you ticket place refeer. I like pot. I like tricking you into talking
about superheros. I don't think it's true that all British people
pronounce it "suburus" Ben. Its just you. The number was one.
I'm sitting down. I'm reading your book so I can't catch you
biting an imaginary toothpick and not looking at me nonstop
like a beautiful loon. Oh, I don't know why one.
Just one. Thanks for the salmon Ben. It was so awful.
Nobody should ever buy salmon at Kings Cross
but thanks for the salmon Ben. Thank you so much!
I tell you holding your wrist like a small warm device
and we are on the train already

Birds in the Engine

I don't feel that hopeless

Dropping my luggage
with reckless abandon

Isn't it funny that there is a monk in the airport?

Everyone is quietly trying to take his picture
without giving themselves up

Cielo Drive

Surprise
         you missed the point again

         You Are
                  Here

down the street behind the street

         driving up house-numbers, down again

forgetting the relator's cement-shaped name

to see if you can feel it

Meanwhile, through all of your abrupt breaking
         & change of song

         the house is itself *unseeable*

I'm told when I'm drunk I get *very opinionated*

         Fuck Manson's music I say, *and Fuck you.*

         Yes, Some mornings

         some poems
         are just a choice

         to flip between stations
         when *Feel Like Makin' Love* comes on.

less so

because of the time with the broken eggs   in your kitchen I took up dance
                                                                          many years later

in the most beginning classes   there is not   even   an accompanist

                    just the tease of ones trained hands
                    in a different room through the hall

          those   men,   who, using their toes evenly on the floor

                                                      in the way   like it is nothing
                              & their less remarkable   wild leaps
this   as if to indicate

                              somewhere you can get to   but also   not that

the best dancers move in such a way   (almost sloppy)
it makes you think   maybe somewhere   a screw is loose   in the perfect
body

I often point my toe & turn   while I wait in San Francisco in the train
station
self acceptance is one evolved form of selfishness
as is the imperfect half-circle

          across the country   I have made thousands

& when his sight went my grandfather left me a protractor and good pens
I let waste
          now it his hard to think of him   without thinking also of money or
objects

I never learned to turn the whole way

                    of course   I never got that far

Brazil

For instance, there is a map and a pistol.
There is a Dodge, a street sign,
a bored gunman calling out
"Try again sweetheart" while
I shakily hold my finger
with my other finger, land
somewhere in the water. It is

what it is. Maybe I'll be taller
in the next life. Different shoe,
narrow foot, ocean instead
of pretend ocean leaking
through some island
the real ocean had planted
inside it.

Cul-de-sac

I remember in the college library
when my friend dropped many bananas on the table
and said I LOVE HAVING ENOUGH OF SOMETHING!!
       but, enough portmanteaus
       & those
       greyly lit
       fragments
       of events
       & sex
I don't care about sex
       except doing it
which is almost always fun
& never too sad or moral to take back

Close Up

That woman's hand
looks like your hand
from a certain angle.

Even once in a while
a waste bin caught fire
& I could see your face
through such blue smoke.

Even now, the beauty isn't lost
before it hits me.

Even the moon,
on its first try, has such
a soft voice.

Weak Language

Tomato: 2/3 water. Certain drinks
will bring my ghosts out. My friend
is trying to videotape a stranger
shooting his book with a gun.
What is so wrong? I may not be the fox
in the fable, but that doesn't make me
the mail girl. Everyone should know
how to make themself cry. I'm sorry
I spilled soup on your keyboard.
So maybe every other moment is
the impossible one to fight off

Centripetal Force

Light scattered over the pool
all morning. I'm not gone

but I'm going in now.
See. You have to plummet
toward the drain like a fruit pit

to see what your god wants
from you. Mark Rothko
painted one self-portrait

titled *self- portrait.* His eyes
are dark eggs. Their seas rise

& turn to steam. I just want
to swim a little further out.

The magic isn't lost on me.

1906

So, the horses run
for a while and become horses again

and so it is Spring, the flood, loose carriage

bulbous to shattered
state of lake

the real version of a thing
is lodged in the middle
of the red herring-thing

and the dimming
Baltic sea

is even dimmer since

over the navy yard

so much time spent making rafts
in the shallow end. 'dead self'
I'm sorry I left you
starved and defenseless
to such ordinary flagellations
of rain. w.c. and his friend with the hat
took me to the top of that building
it was tall & dust-smothered
on the inside. Christies was
supposed to turn it into
an auction house. I'm always
swimming back, rebuilding
one frail device out of kickboards
and foam arms

Pilot Light

Thank you for the box of cookies
called "Compliments." I like things
like that. On the bus from Nogent
to Paris, a nun helped foist my luggage
out of the aisle. I hated France
but I liked cutting through
the hay fields on a bike in the rain
not knowing whether I was feeling it in
the same language. I like that
there are silos everywhere. Mark.
You look cold in your face. You
look so cross with me I can't stand it.
I am going to break into 1000 candles.

Clear Channel

It sounds like someone
trying to breathe through a bag
in private. Hold still.

I'm going to do this
the way a fireman
is supposed to
carry a kitten out. Seizing

your Ruben Studdard-
sized heart before

it gets too light
to hold. You know.
Like someone eating

away an artichoke. Or like
the sun. How things
want to keep going
back and forth

between this life
and the other one.

dysplasia

every member of T.Rex dies in a different, bizarre accident

& I remember so well the night I called Evan about my cervix

drunk walking   barefoot through the road outside the Meadow Lane
house
I did not understand the pathology totally   *the meaning of it*
tiny, immature pieces of the body killing off the rest

tissue   splayed   not infanticide   instead, doing the opposite
        Though For the most part I see *pathos* in landscape's endurance
        its noble, or disgracing suffering
& as the body attacks itself   when I am scared I act small, even awful
In total there were 2 car crashes, 1 heart attack, an incident choking on a
cocktail cherry
we spoke about it lying in bed   & in the morning I left

his bathroom had a boy-shower and a girl mirror when I remember it
though memory is always easy and wonderful   it's naming that hurts
                                                           that takes forever

lost titles

I am thinking of the island
in the middle of the lake
in the middle of the island.

I tried to talk less. I held my body
squinting. The dark houses became thorns
across the toll-road. Shared blame
is a lousy substitute for a shared life.
The open door emits such
chronically lonely sounds. Sorry
for bringing it up again. I am small.

I just can't get past how you put
that amplifier in the car. Those epitaphs
I sunk in the lake last winter. The boy who died.

So I never returned his letter.
You touched my spider bite,
hoping it was a bruise.

I tried to be quiet for years,
just not soon enough
for them to count
is all.

Emerald City

I am afraid that Conan O'Brien
wouldn't like me even a little

and I would like him so much
I would plunge from the roof
like a sick pigeon
and tear away all of my life.
Is that a thing?

—Or its familiar radiance
what we actually want
when we tell our bodies
to attempt worship?

This week, my kitten started shredding
toilet paper rolls. I find them strewn

at dawn, with the carpet's
half-assed elegance
from that one angle:

how it feels like same air, different wind
when it's really the other way

around. or with sunsets.

what you want
doesn't want you.
it wants you

to watch it recede

Sam Waterston

drought, all through the central valley

maybe the poem begins in the middle of the poem

*

    Another Person

There is a kind of distance between myself and myself. There was not always. For the longest time, there was another person—Of course, some parts were separate—

At night, I might try to watch a crime procedural on television and turn it off when I sensed the other person's cold presence nearby: unmoved by the salacious, melancholic private lives of the TV detectives

*

last things first.
weak sky, Amtrack magazine

scenery pooling
sideways.

for the sake of survival,
it is important
to know how to distract yourself
when *a feeling gets a hold of you*

*

      Wheels keep on turning or,
lamely, *I want to know; have you ever seen the rain??*
is, to me, almost interchangeable. Feels like Memphis.
Felt like. keep it to yourself. No use for argument when there's not any
love left to begin with.

*

– Sorry? A little. Mostly from the way he said
his grandfather peeled off a piece of skin as he removed
a Band-Aid. Not because it was sad or gruesome
as we sat on the patio & closed orange umbrella.

                              Dead— no, Permuted Self.
Non ocean after another and another

still haven't written the poem about windmills.
In the museum hallway's halved yellow air
they looked like the most real thing in the world.

But, then this instead. Well, no. not exactly like that. Other things
happened in between.
It was dry. It was grey. There was shadow where figure should be.

*

Law & Order ran for twenty seasons, tying with the live action
series *Gunsmoke* but falling (as of 2013), five seasons short of
The Simpsons. However, the *Law & Order* franchise lives on:
currently, *Law & Order: Special Victims Unit* is in its seventeenth
season. Female lead Mariska Hargitay ranks as television's highest
paid actress, bringing in $500,000 per episode. Other spin-offs
have included *Law & Order: Criminal Intent, Law & Order: Trial
by Jury, Law & Order: UK, Law & Order: L.A.* and *Exiled* (made
for TV *Law & Order* movie). Creator/producer Dick Wolf has
worked on numerous other series including *Miami Vice* and
recent NBC shows *Chicago P.D.* and *Chicago Fire*.

My short-term memory is no good, but of what I remember, I
remember everything.

*

I try to take a video of Evan
with my phone outside the restaurant.
A message reappears on the screen.

When you argue, *I have this compulsive
need to argue back.* (Jack Mccoy)

It's easy to get the words of great men
mixed up with each other. Jesus.
Abraham. Dumbledore. Rilke.

Supposedly, God forgives every cruelty
except the refusal to acknowledge him.

& Noah did not curse himself for bearing witness
or numbly fling his torso at the horses

& ungainly sheep: their strange, surrendering music

eyes & hooves afloat, clipping water

*

He and the cat are sleeping quietly
next to each other. The TV is on low.
His inert body demands no attention.
None of it hurts. None of
it is strange or difficult to hear.

*

Falling asleep separately
after making love
is one measure of distance.

Here is another:
Road, flowers,
shadow-washing road.
Bare-backed implant
palm: bowing through
an apartment-
shaped light

syndicate noise
a remark about weather or money

In the original *Law & Order*, the personal lives of the detectives and
prosecutors were, if not ignored altogether, peripheral to the narrative
of a particular case. The sounds (DOOT, DUN DUN) that accompany
changes of occasion and/or setting have become one of the most iconic
features of the *Law & Order* franchise, portraying the rigidity of the
legal process and allowing directors to link otherwise disparate scenes,
moments, casts, and aspects of the legal process.

The distance between *I love you*
and *I love being with you*
and *I love being inside of you*

*

I always put something on to fall asleep
now. I don't know how I didn't for so long.

What did I do to train myself not to?

*

DUN DUN

I am coming back now.

Partial light in the next room:

There is a specific noise
in the program to signify
a 'change of setting'

DUN DUN

I sweep water on & off my face

It is almost morning

The detectives' dark coats trail softly behind them
As they walk down 23rd street in the snow

Lucy Tiven was born in Manhattan and lives in Los Angeles, where she works as a Staff Writer for ATTN: and Spring Poetry Editor for the Fanzine. She got her B.A. from Kenyon College, where she was the 2013 winner of the John Crowe Ransom Poetry Prize, the American Academy of Poets Prize and 2011 Proper Prize for Poetry. She was a Top Ten Finalist in the 2011 Tennessee Williams Literary Festival. She likes wine and open water and has a sassy back cat named Joey & a little grey cat named Nena.

Her poems have appeared in various literary journals including *Lazy Fascist Review, Hobart, The Quietus, Two Serious Ladies, Dark Fucking Wizard, The Scrambler, Pop Serial,* and *Front Porch* and the anthologies *It's Night in San Francisco but it's Sunny in Oakland* and *40 Likely to Die Before 40: An Introduction to Alt Lit.* She is alive. You can follow her on twitter as @lucytiven.